The Southern Cause
for the love of Dixie

The SOUTHERN CAUSE
for the love of Dixie

THE WAR BETWEEN THE STATES – REENACTORS ON REENACTING

BY THOMAS A. DANIEL

FOREWORD BY JAMES H. COCHRANE, JR.

Brandylane Publishers, Inc.
Richmond, Virginia

Copyright 2008 by Thomas A. Daniel
All rights reserved. This work, or parts thereof, may not be reproduced in any form without written permission from the publisher.

Brandylane Publishers, Inc.
Richmond, Virginia
www.brandylanepublishers.com

Layout / Design by Thomas Trenz

ISBN 978-1-883911-67-6
       1-883911-67-2

Library of Congress Control Number: 2007943231

This book is dedicated to Ted Potter, Francis Fralin, Amy Moorefield,
John Yau and Margaret Porter.

Thanks
TD

FROM THE PUBLISHER

In an effort to preserve the natural, spontaneous language of the reenactors interviewed for *The Southern Cause*, Thomas Daniel recorded and transcribed the interviews, and the editors made only slight grammatical changes for clarification.

The points of view expressed herein do not necessarily represent the views of Brandylane Publishers, Inc.

Captain James H. Cochrane, Jr., Richmond, Virginia 2007

FOREWORD

by James H. Cochrane, Jr.

For me, it all began back on the 21st of July 1961: this passion, sometimes obsession, that I have for Confederate military "living history." On that hot Saturday afternoon upon the hallowed grounds of the Manassas National Battlefield Park, I witnessed for the first time, a month before my eighth birthday, wave after wave of charging infantry and cavalry, all accompanied by the thunder of artillery and numerous loud renditions of the Rebel Yell. This was a very special occasion as it was held exactly 100 years to the day after the first bloody melee that took place along the banks of Bull Run in Prince William County, Virginia. Shortly after the recreated display of valor and duty was over, my father took me to the rows of vendors that were present, where I had him purchase my first set of plastic gray and blue soldier figurines.

I have been playing war ever since. The endless hours of self-designed scenarios that followed only added to my curiosity and interest in the period known to some as the War Between the States, to others as the American Civil War, the War of Northern Aggression, the Second American Revolution, the War for Southern Independence, or the Late Unpleasantness.

I was lucky enough to have Dr. James I. Robertson, Jr. as a mentor in my sophomore year at Virginia Polytechnic Institute and State University. Having already been deemed a C.P. Miles Distinguished Professor of History, there was no one else in the world of academia who could surpass "Bud" Robertson on the subject of The War. Under his tutelage, I gained a renewed interest in my Confederate roots. While working as a volunteer at the Museum of the Confederacy on the committee to put on the institution's first membership-raising ball, I was given the task of securing "living historians" who would set up an encampment on the ball's site at Tredegar Ironworks in downtown Richmond, and acquiring the necessary permits from the local fire marshal for both musket fire and artillery shoots. I got to know the members of the artillery unit that portrayed Reilly's Battery from Raleigh, North Carolina and decided to model a new organization after them.

With the delivery of "Big John," a Parrott ten-pounder in May of 1998, my artillery unit was off and running. Since one of my Confederate ancestors, John Binford Knibb, was an artillerist from Goochland County, Virginia, I decided to name the unit (as well as the Parrott) after him. Within the next eight years, Knibb's battery had acquired a 24-pound Coehorn mortar, two three-inch ordnance rifles, a smoothbore Napoleon twelve-pounder, two Tredegar mountain rifles, a full-scale mountain horwitzer, a half-scale mountain horwitzer, a "Pack Parrott" rifle, and a Gatling Gun. The membership had grown to over seventy men, women, and children who hailed from Michigan, Ohio, Florida, South Carolina, North Carolina, Maryland, Pennsylvania, Virginia, and West Virginia. For the most part, my fellow reenactors are family to me. We burn powder together, sweat together, endure the harshest elements nature can throw at us together.

The question, "Why do you reenact?" was posed to me by photographer, Thomas A. Daniel, who created this book. It is through the art form of living history that we, as descendants of those who endured that fearful period of time, can hope to retell the story in an accurate and factual way to the present generation of Americans, to their children and again to their children. Finally, one of the more important reasons for reenacting is to support battlefield preservation. More and more "living history" events are donating a portion of their proceeds to help save sacred space from the jaws of developers and other societal encroachment. This participation by event producers in the effort to save these lands brings the reenactor even closer to the past and to the land.

It has been said that the eyes are the window to the soul. This seems to be quite true as you peer upon the faces of the living historians in the pages to follow. Many of them, if not most, perform their recreational pastime with the same diligence, beliefs and sense of duty as their forefathers. It also seems that these folks are not just actors, but reincarnated spirits from the past whose memories still haunt them: the carnage on the battlefield, the suffering in the field and convalescing hospitals and the destitution of the Southern home front. This form of leisure, however, is not just for those of us with ancestral connections. Many of the present-day Johnny Rebs and Billy Yanks do not have direct blood lineage to an American sailor or soldier that fought in the early 1860s. These people mostly "fight" to keep our history alive as well as to enjoy the life "in the field" just like today's great grandsons and great granddaughters of the Confederate and Union veterans.

The photographs were taken at reenactments in Brooksville near the West Coast of Florida, in Aiken in south-central South Carolina, on the original battlefield at Bentonville in North Carolina, Secessionville just outside of Charleston, South Carolina, on the grounds at Endview Plantation between Newport News and Yorktown, Virginia and on Cedar Creek Battlefield at numerous sites, including that of Belle Grove Plantation. Whether your allegiances lie with either the South or the North, I hope that you enjoy the photographs and words that follow and that they may inspire you to become a part of the world of living history.

James H. Cochrane, Jr.

TIMELESSNESS
Carol Jenkins, 1st Peninsula Artillery

The past speaks with echoes traveling winds of time and space

There are those who hear these voices as they weave through fine old lace

And reenact the battles of the valiant fight for life

To survive the field, hunger and cold

While spirits play the drum and fife

Feel them all around you

And hear their victory songs

See them waving their flag

And march through cannon fog

Some lessons are expensive

Our nation had to learn

Let nothing threaten brotherhood

Peace on this land was earned.

Spend time with these folks,

Trust them with your love and bow your heads to pray,

That history only repeats itself in this pleasing, harmless way

And the winds of time blow gently into the brave new day.

ACKNOWLEDGMENTS

My first thank you goes to the reenactors who have for several reasons pursued this particular hobby. Many honor ancestors who fought in the War Between the States, and are fascinated with uniforms, weapons, tactics, and pursue every part of this hobby in detail. Many reenact for the comradery: the good times sitting around the campfire. Many relish the noise, smoke, and heat that comes with action on the field. A handful, I fear, are still fighting The War. A multitude of these people reenact, according to Civil War historian Nicky Hughes, to "educate the people."

I would like to thank Tom Trenz and Robert Pruett of Brandylane Publishers, Inc. for taking this on, Melissa Christenson for being my assistant, Margaret Porter-Daniel for her endless support and for writing about the ball. I would also like to thank Chaplain Wally Hudgins, Artillery, Col. Joe Ferguson, Cavalry, and Col. Shoemake, Infantry, for getting me outside the wire. Thanks to Bill Vincent for my first uniform, as well as Paulette and Lt. Col. Dwight Nesbitt for looking out for me. To Col. Faranelli, a brother in arms who befriended me: thank you. I would like to acknowledge Capt. Jimmy Cochrane Artillery for writing the foreword, Civil War historian Nicky Hughes, and Medford Taylor for his creative editing. And, of course, to all the troops in Knibb's Battery: you are family. Thank You.

To all who reenact The War Between the States,
from the heart, this is for you.

God bless,

2nd Lt. Thomas A. Daniel
War Correspondent, ANV Artillery Staff

INTRODUCTION

BY THOMAS A. DANIEL

THE SOUTHERN CAUSE:
FOR THE LOVE OF DIXIE

"The Cause of the South was the love of my youth and I shall love it to the end"

Quote from Mrs D. Giraud Wright,
Real Daughters of the Confederacy

In my youth, my Aunt Gertie would tell stories of great grandfather Fidus Rink and how his brothers and his fortune were lost in the War Between the States. She told how he always honored his bond with his fellow soldiers forged in battle and death; fought more for the love of his state, North Carolina, and comradeship of fellow North Carolinians.

So when the *H.L. Hunley*, a Confederate submarine, was found in Charleston Harbor in 2004, I knew I had to go pay tribute to those men who gave their lives as testimony to their inherent idealism and belief in something greater than self. I watched, fascinated as hundreds came dressed in Civil War era clothes. Confederate and Union soldiers marched in order accompanied by women dressed in mourning clothes. They followed the caisson in earnest sorrow as they marched to the cemetery to salute the brave men of the *Hunley*. I saw tears in the reenactors' eyes and felt a bond. I too had lost family and joined unexpectedly in the mournful salute. A question I had always asked myself now had to be answered. "Why do people reenact the epic War Between the States? Why relive such a tragic and bloody time in our history?"

I have addressed this question in today's spirit of that time not to recreate the battles, the reasons or try to decide who really won and lost. I joined with the men and women of Knibb's Battery, the 140th regiment of Lee's Northern Virginia Army. As their "war correspondent," I have traveled the South to photograph and interview participants, be they Northerners, Southerners, Native American or African-American. From each have been stories that range from loving to dress up or playing "cowboys and Indians," to remembrance of the "truth," and for some an emotional tie to the ancestor who died on the battlefield.

The Southern Cause: For the Love of Dixie is a testimony of living historians to a time and place in history.

THOMAS BAKER
2ND LIEUTENANT COMMANDER

SCV Magruder-Ewell Camp #99
Newport News, Virginia

My mother's kinfolk fled Germany about 1610 under religious persecution. Seeking safety and freedom, they found their way to the Carolinas of America. At present their history is incomplete, for her family suffered greatly under heil Sherman.

My father's kinfolk also appear in the Carolinas (North Carolina) by mid-1700, possibly earlier, from Scotland. These records are also presently incomplete, for they too suffered under heil Sherman.

We do know that my great grandfather watched over the families and farms while a band of my great uncles and cousins rostered and served at Fort Fisher in Wilmington, NC. There they served the entire war and all survived the assaults and were forced to surrender upon that final hill, valiantly atop Buchanans Battery on January 15, 1865. Others who rostered in NC, served on both NC and VA battlefields. Both families were poor immigrant planters within this new nation of kindreds. Serving in their Christian faith, they, along with the Southern collective, became the pillars of our heritage. From y'all to bluegrass, they are the founders of our Beloved Homeland Dixie.

Following the command of Christ and Gen. Stephen D. Lee, I joined to vindicate our peoples' honor and truth. Honor to the honorable and freedom to all through the truth. This is why I serve in the Sons of Confederate Veterans under the colors of the most beautifully designed flag ever sewn which is the full symbol, psalm, and reflection of our heritage, culture and homeland.

THOMAS BAKER'S HISTORY
FOR THE SONS OF CONFEDERATE VETERANS

Our camp serves the lower peninsula and is located at what was one of the most volatile frontlines during our struggle for independence. Gen. John Baukhead Magruder and Col. Benjamin Stoddard Ewell are the two Southern heroes our camp is named for. Today we are under the honorable command of Commander Gary G. Bruce. Our camp was established in Williamsburg, Virginia prior to June 10, 1889 as Magruder-Ewell Camp #36 United Confederate Veterans.

June of 1900 our camp erected a monument in Greenlawn Cemetery, Newport News, Virginia, to honor the mass re-burial of 163 compatriot soldiers. These men were prisoners of war who were all left to die and buried in Butcher Butler prison camp, also in downtown Newport News. All were basically murdered for refusing to sign a revisionist oath of allegiance.

Oct. 26, 1903. The veteran soldier, Pvt. William James Adams, is the last camp commander before they were disbanded as UCV Camp #36.

May 5, 1929. The camp is chartered as SCV, but again goes into a lull for a lack of membership participation.

April 1, 1975. The camp is reactivated as SCV Magruder-Ewell Camp #99 under the leadership of 1st commander Col. Robert S. Coleman, who is still very active with the camp today. Our camp has grown again thanks to Col. Coleman. We now have about 100 current members with a color guard to participate and serve in numerous directives and events. We have committees for a number of civic activities and historical and current activism. We are also blessed with our local Bethel Chapter UDC, a real fine bouquet of Confederate ladies with whom to serve the Southern Cause.

Hollywood Cemetery - 2005

THE H.L. HUNLEY

The *H.L. Hunley* was a non-commissioned submarine of the Confederate States Navy and was the first of its kind to sink a warship. It was built at Mobile, Alabama and was shipped by rail to Charleston, South Carolina. On February 17, 1864, *Hunley* attacked a small sailing warship, the steam-powered *USS Housatonic* in Charleston harbor. After sinking the Union ship, *Hunley* also sank and took all eight crewmen to a watery grave. The wreck was recovered from Charleston harbor August 8, 2000. On April 17, 2004, the eight crewmen were interred with full military honors in Charleston's Magnolia Cemetery. Although the identity of the comma nder has long been known to be George E. Dixon, the identities of the other crewmembers remained a mystery until the remains were recovered and DNA testing identified the three American-born of the crew. The other four crewmen were of European origin and have been harder to identify. Researchers were also pleased to discover a misshapen $20 gold piece, minted in 1860 in the area close to Lt. Dixon. It had an inscription that read, "My life preserver." Forensics then found a healed injury to Lt. Dixon's hipbone, confirming a family legend that Dixon's sweetheart had given him the coin to protect him and it had indeed in the Battle of Shiloh where he was wounded on April 16, 1862. A bullet struck the coin in his pocket, saving his leg and possibly his life, after which he had it engraved, and carried it as a lucky charm. The following photographs (on pages 3,4,5,) lay witness to this sentiment to the Southern Cause.

Information compiled by Melissa Christenson

TRIBUTE TO *H.L. HUNLEY* - APRIL 17, 2004

BURIAL MARCH OF 8 *H.L. HUNLEY* SOLDIERS - APRIL 2004

H.L. Hunley 8 soldiers, Magnolia Cemetery - Charleston, South Carolina - April 2004

HONOR GUARD - BATTLE OF BIG BETHEL - ENDVIEW, VIRGINIA 2005
Front Row (L-R): William Wells, Curtis Hicks, Chris Liesman; Back Row: James Jasper, Thomas Hayman, Ken Blanton, Thomas Baker, Jason Keithley, Jesse Gundry

Three Confederates - Richmond, Kentucky 2005

61ST VIRGINIA INFANTRY: BATTLE OF BIG BETHEL - ENDVIEW, VIRGINIA 2005
led by Sgt. John Strayer (Far Right)

Hunters Raid - Lexington, Virginia 2005

Ron Pierce, Captain of the 32nd Virginia (left)

I'm in it because my ancestors fought in the Civil War from 1861-1865. From 1864-1865, one was a Union prisoner of war. So, I just enjoy doing it. I have been doing it eleven years now. I think the Southern Cause was hopeless but the guys never gave up. I give them credit for that.

Tony Reguni, First Sergeant with the 32nd Virginia (right)

The coat that I'm wearing is a Confederate coat, called a Richmond gray shell jacket. A lot of Confederates didn't always wear gray, like my pants are called a curvy blue; a lot of them wore it. I'm into it too because my great-great grandfather was in the Confederate artillery and I've always loved history. My great-great grandpa's name was John S. Webber; he was a sergeant with the Richmond Fayette artillery. My great-great grandfather wrote in a history book that the lieutenant was writing a letter home telling his family that he wished that the Yankees would attack because his men needed coats. So I guess if they didn't have no coats and they needed to be warm they would have put that blue coat on to stay warm, especially that late in the war, I mean they were probably in rags. That is written in the regimental history book in a letter. I've been able to actually stand on the very spots where that unit was in different battles. Fredericksburg, it's called House In The Hills. If you go up there, there's guns up there right now. His unit was there. They were here at Windsmill, at McGruder, they were over at Gloucester Point, they were at Petersburg. Then there is my family on my mother's side: my great-great grandpa was Confederate artillery and his father and brother were in the Union navy. So they came from Norfolk, the same family, and they were split. Sometimes it was just where your loyalty was and what you believed in. I never heard anything about them having slaves so it was just about what they believed in.

BATTLE OF BIG BETHEL - ENDVIEW, VIRGINIA 2005

AL STONE
General Robert E. Lee - Army of Northern Virginia

One of the most frequent questions posed to me during the last fifteen years is: "Why do you do this – reenacting thing, portraying General Robert E. Lee?" I must confess, it is for selfish reasons!

As a youth growing up on a dairy farm in New York State, I was indoctrinated in our nation's history by my father who was engrossed in Revolutionary War history; to him, that was probably one of the most important subjects that he could discuss, after all, many of the events surrounding that era took place in the area where we lived. The War Between the States was something remote, occurring in the South by those people whom we were all led to believe were traitors—at least that's what we were told by teachers who received their information from the history books, that were written by Northerners and published by Northern presses.

I guess I began to realize there was another side to the story when I relocated to Lynchburg, Virginia in April 1965. At that time, there were many observances celebrating the 100th anniversary of the conclusion of the contest and I was right in the middle of it, residing about twenty-five miles from Appomattox itself. I had occasions to speak with children of actual participants of the contest and in one case enjoyed several conversations with a former slave lady who was born in 1853; she could recall with some vividness the war and the conditions that existed at the time. While residing in Lynchburg, the War came to life for me and from that time on I began a study that culminated with aligning myself with reenactors in 1990.

I didn't start out with the intent of studying any particular aspect, but the contest in general. However, one cannot study the war long before recognizing that one of the principal characters was in fact General Robert E. Lee. As an advisor to President Jefferson Davis initially, he assumed command of the Army of Northern Virginia in June 1862 and from that point, he and that army were forces to be reckoned with. In a few short weeks he forced Union forces to retreat from the Virginia peninsula then went on to rout the Yankee Army from Manassas Junction for the second time and held the Union Army at bay on the shores of the Antietam Creek near Sharpsburg, Maryland, and all the while outnumbered at least two to one. Over the next two and a half years he continued to lead his army to many victories but in the end could not overcome overwhelming numbers and resources and capitulated to General U. S. Grant on April 9, 1865 in the little southern town of Appomattox, Virginia.

While Lee, Jefferson Davis, and the many others aligned themselves with what they deemed to be a just cause, they were branded traitors because they did not support the Union effort, which in actuality was contradictory to the United States Constitution as set forth by our nation's founding fathers. And this is what I was beginning to learn. Having studied the contest and its causes, I now became aware of the real issues that brought on the war. Under the guise of "implied powers," the established "Federal" government had become a "National" government, usurping the rights of the individual states as guaranteed by the constitution.

As "living historians," thousands provide an accurate insight on the contest and what led up to it. After intensive study, they attire themselves in period clothing and on a regular basis camp under similar conditions, meeting and speaking with hundreds of thousands of listeners in an effort to keep our nation's history alive in an accurate manner. In association with other members of Lee's Lieutenants, I have the opportunity to teach history. We as a group have studied our characters, the war and enjoy presenting the information to those who are willing to listen.

Over many decades, hundreds of thousands have given to the last full measure, in an effort to preserve the freedoms guaranteed by our founding fathers in the original constitution and it is for us to bear that report to those who come after us. Can we do any less? Should we do any less?

Hunters Raid, Lexington, Virginia 2005

LEE'S LIEUTENANTS

Seated Left to Right

Name:	Portraying:
Al Stone	General Robert E. Lee
Jim Pencs	General Thomas J. Jackson

Standing Left to Right

Dennis Cole	General Lewis Armistead
Ron Cole	General John B. Gordon
Jim Choate	General George Pickett
Joe Ferguson	Major Joe Ferguson
Mike Mehaffey	General Jubal Early
Jack Maples	General Montgomery D. Corse
Jimmy Boykin	Major Robert W. Hunter
Carl Stewart	Capt. Frank Armistead

Standing Rear

Gary Allen	Lt. Col. Charles Taylor

Absent From Photo

Jay Vogel	General James Longstreet
David Blosser	General John B. Hood
David Trimble	General Isaac Trimble
Niles Clark	General John Brown

Lee's Lt's - Dixie Days, Mechanicsville, Virginia 2005

LEON VAUGHAN
Private, 54th Massachusetts voluntary infantry company B, Union

Well, supposedly the southern states wanted to do as they pleased without interference from the central government. That included a whole lot of things, trade, slavery was one of them, and they just simply wanted more states' rights than central government rights. The Southern Cause still lives. I see it in my reenactment events every time, and not only that, when I travel throughout the South, sure. It doesn't offend me. If I was very shaky about my own identity and everything it would be. But when you are confident in who you are and what you are, you are not intimidated. Before asking people about the flag you have to ask the people do they know what the flag is, because the battle flag is not the Confederate flag and they are talking about the battle flag and not the Confederate flag.

Pocahontas Park, Virginia 2005

CHARLES WILLIS,
from Fayetteville, NC.
Battery B, Second Regimen, U.S. CT's Light Artillery

I personally went down to Columbia, South Carolina when the whole flag incident took place, ok the very beginning, I guess seven or eight years ago. I was there; people were asking me, because there was one, two blacks there. "Why are you here?" Because I understand history. I also understand the history of the flag. I also know that there has been some errors made on both sides, and you're not always right, you may be a leader but you can be off. I understand the history of the flag. I understand that the flag was misused, and by being a teacher and a history major, I just have to take it the way it is. History is good, bad, and ugly. Sometimes you're not going to like it. I know the Southern Cause still lives. I see it in teaching. I teach in the middle school. I see the pride that people have in their ancestors and I know the pride I have in my own ancestors and I can just be perfectly honest with you, it should be that way. This is history, and as I said before, it's good, bad, and ugly. But people can't forget their relatives, sometimes they may want to, and some of them will tell you they're not sure, but they're still yours and you still claim them no matter what.

POCAHONTAS PARK, VIRGINIA 2005

CAROL JENKINS'S GROUP: 1ST PENINSULA

Top to Bottom, L-R: 1st Lt. Bill Dropski, Pvt. Kenzy Joyner, Prt. Kathy Hare, Carol Jenkins, Pvt. Scott Smith, Pvt. Gary Peters, Pvt. Jeffery Quieato, Pvt. Ray Crafton, Cpl. Michael White, Pvt. Mike Smith, 1st Sgt. Mark Janser, Pvt. Robin Nipper, Col. Tom Foster, Pvt. Chrissy Maul, 2nd Lt. Russell Jenkins, Pvt. Henry Howe, Cpl. Billy Dopski

Corporal James B. Dunn (a.k.a. BirdDog) with horse, Mary Ghost - Pocahontas Park, Virginia 2005

BERTRAM HAYES VINSON, JR.

At this writing, my son, Bertram Hayes Vinson III, is serving as a medic in the Combat Engineers, Iraq. My grandson, Bertram Hayes Vinson IV "Bo", and I went to Shiloh. We took the government fifty cent tour. A big deal was made about all the federal troops having their own marker. After the tour, my grandson Bo said, "Papa, where are our boys buried?" I took him over on the other side of the park to a big single mass grave. It did have a big marker. I pointed out to the site and said, "They're over there." His comment was, "Papa, they don't have numbers like the federals." I told him, "We lost." His comment was, "But Papa, we should have markers too!" I told him I agreed, but we lost. The wisdom and understanding of a fourteen-year-old boy out does all the "politically correct." His statement brings tears to my eyes to this day. "But Papa, they were soldiers too." Not North, not South, not Union, not Confederate, but "soldiers."

Bo & B.H. Vinson Jr., Knibb's Battery, Gettysburg, Virginia

Battle of Big Bethel, Endview Planation, Virginia 2005

Two Young Soldiers - Lexington, Virginia 2005

TWO GUNS
1st Maryland Battalion Cavalry and 1st Lt. of Battery B

We're actually a detachment to 1st Maryland and we started out as 2nd Maryland artillery and we all went South while 1st Maryland's artillery all went North.

I like to teach the kids living history because if we don't teach them, no one will. The best part is blowing stuff up with big guns, and that's it! Like having Fourth of July, twelve times a year.

Two Guns at 1st Bull Run

WOUNDED CONFEDERATE SOLDIER - CEDAR CREEK, VIRGINIA

Appomattox, Virginia 2004

Confederate Charge - Secessionville, South Carolina 2004

Union Charge - 1st Bull Run - Manassas, Virginia 2005

BURNING OF AIKEN, SOUTH CAROLINA 2004

BURNING OF AIKEN, SOUTH CAROLINA 2004

BRANCH WHITE, LYNN WELTON
Chesterfield Light Artillery

I do love the history and feel I'm helping to keep the heritage alive in a time when people are trying to dismantle it. Reenacting and shooting cannon are so much fun. It reminds me of when we were kids visiting all the battlefields and running through the breastworks while shooting Yankees with our makeshift muskets. It's even more fun now because we use cannons and real gunpowder! My fiancée, Lynn Welton, started re-enacting because she said if she didn't, she would never see me!

Cedar Creek, Virginia 2005

PRIVATE SUSAN MCKNIGHT
4th VA Calvary Company D
Little Fork Rangers

We reenact for lots of reasons. Southern pride is a huge thing. It's also about education, being able to teach people what really happened. The sad thing is that they don't really know because a lot of schools are not teaching it the way that it should be taught, so that's what we are doing. Preserving battlefields is also a big deal. In this day and time they are in danger of being developed and built on. What Tom is doing here is also a great service. Thanks for everything, man.

Battle of Big Bethel - Endview Plantation, Virginia 2005

Ellison Brothers - 1st Manassas, Virginia 2006

Pvt. Richard Turner, Knibb's Battery - Cedar Creek, Virginia 2006

DAVE JOHNSON
4th VA, Company D

I ask, "Why would a black man ride with the Confederates?" He says, "I'm gonna tell you like I told the history teacher on living history day at Culpeper High School who asked me the same thing in front of his class. (Puts hat back on—in character.) He looks straight in my eye: "My master gave me two mules and forty acres of land to work on my own, as a free man. I heard an army from the north was gonna come down and take that away from me, and no one was gonna take that from me. So I fought to keep my two mules and forty acres."

Kelly's Ford, Virginia 2005

CAPTAIN DAMN IT
1st Peninsula

The Southern Cause, it ain't dead yet, we just getting started good. The Southern Cause is a state of mind I think. Personally, I don't think any Southerner would ever admit to the war being over with yet. No I don't think it's a lost cause, it may be dwarfed at the moment or something like that, but I don't know, maybe until the federal government starts bagging off with some of the bullshit… the Southern Cause will always be around. I love to reenact; when the gun starts going off and the smoke gets back in my face, it's a rush that nothing else can give me. I've never touched the real thing though, as close as this, is about as close as I'll ever get, I have a feeling. I definitely love Dixie. The flag gets a bad rep because you've got other groups that use the battle flag for non-traditional methods. Other than the battle flag, nobody seems to know what any of the other flags mean.

BATTLE OF BIG BETHEL - ENDVIEW PLANTATION, VIRGINIA 2005

AUSTIN TWO FEATHERS
Cherokee Mounted Rifles

I'm actually Notaweegan and Irish. We fought on the side of the South. We fought when we felt like fighting and if we weren't fighting we might sneak around and raid the Union. We had Cherokee mounted with rifles, we had Colonials, we even had Generals. Cherokee Mounted Rifles was our unit. I love to reenact, It's part of my heritage. Anything I can get for American Indians out there for people to see, I'm gonna do it. I'm mostly Native; I'm a card carrier. It's a tribe from basically Ohio right now. We're known as Northern Indians or French Indians. I'm the only native American reenactor I know of right now. I've heard of some others but I have not come up upon them yet.

Battle of Big Bethel - Endview Plantation, Virginia 2005

JOE TOPINKA: CUSTER
from Bedford, PA
Portraying George Armstrong Custer

I do this to bring history to life. I live the life that George Armstrong Custer lived because he was a legend in his time but ahead of his time as well. He went above and beyond the call of duty to make sure the job was done. The job being to preserve the Union of the United States of America.

Question asked by author Thomas Daniel: He was accused of killing a lot of Indians unnecessarily?

He had false reconnaissance on the whereabouts of the Indians and didn't have all of his ducks in a row…the Indians surrounded him…Well, it was a bad call.

aka. General Custer - 1st Bull Run, Manassas, Virginia 2005

THE BALL

The giant tents are luminous in the night. They float in the field with one tent near the Confederate encampment and one across the hill next to the Union encampment. People are driving in from afar and others are catching shuttle buses from the camps to the Ball tents. There are gowns of extraordinary beauty and detail and then there are field dresses with modest skirts made of uncomplicated cotton. The uniforms come studded with gold buttons and braid on long frock coats and then there are simple shirts with suspendered pants. Every layer, every decadence of society is joined with the simple and modest and we all come together under one huge tent.

    The music starts. Fiddles quicken the pace and traditional instruments from the 1800s weave in and out of the dance calls. A gentleman in mad hatter attire calls the dances while his daughter and wife circle around the dancers to help them with the steps. Light, music and laughter fill the air as we do-si-do, spin, arch and promenade our way through the night.

Margaret Porter-Daniel

The Ball at Cedar Creek, Virginia 2006

THE BALL AT CEDAR CREEK, VIRGINIA 2006

THE BALL AT CEDAR CREEK, VIRGINIA 2006

REGGIE ROBERTS
Ordnance Sgt.
Knibb's Battery

The Civil War was never dry history to me. In my home were books with photographs of all the Confederate generals and other scenes of the era.

My Grandmother Hill was born in 1854 and was ten years old when the war ended. Both Grandfather Roberts and Grandfather Hill were born in 1841. Both were veterans of the war. I knew Granny Hill well and remember her funeral when I was five. Elcany Roberts was in the 50th NC infantry and John Hill was in a NC company of the 62nd Georgia Cavalry. Both units were from Wayne County, North Carolina.

Even before Sherman's march, eastern North Carolina saw considerable action as federal forces occupied the port towns and sent raids inland, foraging and looting.

The history books were filled with dates and major battles, but my childhood view of the war was on a more immediate and personal level.

As a longtime member of the Richmond Civil War Roundtable, I studied the war on a different level. I always had an interest in artillery and its history. When an opportunity presented itself to join a Civil War battery, I was ready. My experience in reenacting has given me more of an insider's view of the war and what they actually did as well as a deep appreciation of the hardships they endured in their struggle for independence.

CEMETERY - HENRICO, VIRGINIA 2006

Captain Ed Craun
Chief of Engineering,
Army Northern Virginia Staff Artillery

I reenact for the camraderie and the friendship of people who want to keep history alive. I believe to honor my ancestors is to live as they did over 150 years ago. If you don't learn from history, you are doomed to repeat it.

Secessionville, South Carolina 2006

MIKE MEHAFFEY
General Early

Why do we do what we do? Why do we put on those hot wool uniforms and try to bring the Civil War back to life? Hey, you, the South lost the war—let it go, get over it!

How many times have I heard those questions (and others like them) asked? How often do I encounter people that are ignorant of the history of the Civil War and care absolutely nothing about the subject other than to be critical of it and yes, us?

I enjoy talking with people that may ask similar questions but are truly eager to learn something. They don't have to take my word on any given subject but maybe I have given them enough that with a little research they can answer the questions for themselves.

My wife Leslie and I have been a part of reenacting for eleven years now. I have been for most of that time in artillery. We have been the owners of a 12-pounder Napoleon cannon for the past five years. And that means that on top of uniforms, equipment, tents, etc., we had to purchase a trailer to carry the gun. Once it is fully loaded, the half-ton pickup couldn't handle the weight, so we had to purchase a ton truck to pull it. Back to the old question of why do we do it? That's a lot of money (and time) invested there, ain't it?

Well obviously, we don't do this in hopes of making any money by it. No, we do this in honor of our ancestors who fought and died for a cause they believed in. A cause that yes, was lost, but they endured the hardships and the heartache, and death and destruction. We do it so that the *history* of this war—the real history—will live on.

We do our research so that we can effectively teach others. Schools of today do not teach any Civil War history. When I was in grade school (early 60s) the section about the war took six weeks to go through. Today, in high school, it takes the amount of time allotted to read three pages!?! What can anyone learn about something so complex as the Civil War in only three pages?

I guess that because the politically correct ideal has so taken over everything these days it would be unthinkable to teach our young people that at least 60,000 *black* men wore a *gray* uniform (that figure is, at the last I heard, documented) and many of those same men were armed. But wait! The war was over nothing but slavery!?! How could you put a gun into the hands of someone that so hated the white man?

Think about that. And don't forget that ugly, hate-filled flag! That same flag that flew for the purpose of supporting slavery! Now, why do you suppose that such ignorance as that is talked about today? Why do you suppose that the sight of this flag causes so much anguish to so many people today? Could it possibly be that, as I stated earlier, three pages in the history book doesn't cover such topics? Plus the fact that most of the politically correct crowd doesn't know the difference between the "Stars and Bars" (1st National) and the flag about which I am referring, the battle flag. And the fact that the battle flag didn't come into existence until *after* the *first* battle at Manassas and was intended for just that—a battle flag—one that Southern troops could see and readily know where their lines were?

And because, just maybe, some simple-minded, bottom-feeding, scum-sucking, white trash hate groups, take on this beloved flag, a flag that so many honorable men fought and died under—and call it "Theirs"???

And maybe, just maybe, the individuals I mentioned earlier, the ones that don't know and don't care find it easier to hear the rhetoric of these hate groups and somehow relate that into being "history."

Appomattox, Virginia 2006

Cabell F. Willis - Funeral for four soldiers, 2005

Tom Brew, Knibb's Battery - Appomattox, Virginia 2005

SANDY BREW
Knibb's Battery

In a word, it's magic. Many a fantasy has been based on time and travel. In this hobby that fantasy becomes real. Whatever role you choose to practice; you do the research; get the look and mannerisms down and you become a believable persona. You make that person "live" again. We then use these personas to share with the public, via educational activities, a time long ago.

On a personal level, my husband Tom and I also bring our real life medical knowledge into the camp to give back to the hobby by serving the reenactors should the need arise. We handle the small stuff from our first aid kit, monitor those with chronic conditions, and if necessary send for the paramedics.

Lastly, it's the idea of participating in the romance of a society that is long past but still flavors our present day society. Many a young lady has dreamed of being the "belle of the ball," and many a young man has dreamed of being the "hero of the battle."

Appomattox, Virginia 2005

FRANCES M. HUDGINS
Knibb's Battery

Why I joined the United Daughters of the Confederacy (UDC) and Knibb's Battery...

In November 1966, I met someone who I later learned was what is often referred to as a "Civil War Buff." Our relationship grew and we enjoyed doing many of the same things. Many of our Sunday afternoon "dates" involved visiting the battlefield museums and parks in and around Virginia. After watching many living history demonstrations, I often jokingly commented that I felt I could load and fire a musket with my eyes closed. We were married in July 1969. Soon after that, we went to Gettysburg and spent some time touring that hallowed ground. As time passed, we joined several community activities/organizations; it is in our nature to get actively involved. This is not to say that we lost interest in the War Between the States; we just didn't have time to devote to it.

After we both completed our working careers, our interest stirred again. My husband had considered joining the SCV (Sons of Confederate Veterans) for many years, but he hadn't done it. Of course, much of his interest was generated by the fact that his grandfather had participated in the Battle of Chancellorsville in 1863, serving in the Army of Northern Virginia under General Robert E. Lee. My husband joined the J.E.B. Stuart Camp in October 2004. Because of our well established lifestyle of doing things together, it was only natural that I began seeking information about the UDC. I learned from a cousin who had done extensive research of our family tree that I had a great-great grandfather who was captured at Yellow Tavern at the time that General Stuart was mortally wounded; he served time as a POW in Elmira, New York. With this information, I soon pursued my possibilities of joining the UDC. I became a member of the Richmond-Stonewall Jackson Chapter in November 2004.

These activities just led to further involvement. It is one thing to be a member of an organization, attend meetings, do the necessary formalities, and listen to a speaker reflecting on some aspect of the War Between the States. It is another thing to dress in period clothes and reenact the "real" thing. There is no better way to experience this than to be a member of Knibb's Battery. My husband is a part of the artillery battery and I am a civilian in the camp.

So, why do we do these things that may seem unnecessary in the big picture of life? It is very simple. It is because of our ancestors and their contribution to the Southern Cause. I can't imagine what my great-great grandfather endured, particularly while being a POW. But he survived that and returned to his home in Halifax County, Virginia, where he married and raised a family. Among their children, they had a baby girl who would be my great grandmother, who then had a baby boy: my grandfather...my mother's father. Without my great-great grandfather's stamina and perseverance, none of this would have ever happened. Yes, my mother had a baby girl. Me! Is there any wonder why I would honor my Confederate heritage and my great-great grandfather and what he gave during his lifetime. I thank him for what he and many, many other Confederate soldiers and their families sacrificed for our South.

Hollywood Cemetery - Richmond, Virginia 2005

CAPTAIN MARK SHEEHAN

With Virginia's rich history, I couldn't help begin reenacting with my wife, Patty. We've learned so much over the years and are able to interact effectively with the public. We enjoy traveling with our cannon Malachi, named after the biblical prophet. We've been so fortunate to have met some great people from all over the country. Battles, living histories, parades, ceremonies and dances; it is the true enjoyment of the experience and the people we meet.

Longstreet's Corps - Stribbling's Battery, Virginia 2005

FRANK BRENNAN
Knibb's Battery

The Southern Cause lives because the South is a whole brotherhood down here. The South is doing a whole lot better than the North is because the South works together. Every state works together and as they did that before, they're still doing it now. There's politics in the North, there's politics in the South, what's the difference? They're fighting in the North, we ain't down here. There are some discrepancies that certain states hoarded supplies and that led to our downfall but the railroad was knocked out. Then everything we sent on a wagon train to our troops was robbed by the Union. For instance, the guns that came out of Tredegar Ironworks, thirty-six of 'um was made, were shipped out. You know how many of them the South got? Three. The Union got the rest of 'um because they hit the wagon trains, they hit the supply lines. That's it, that's the bottom line. Our lack of supplies was the result of the North's treachery.

Gettysburg, Pennsylvania 2006

COL. JOE FERGUSON
Division Staff
4th Virginia Cavalery

I remember when my kids were knee high and we'd be around the campfire talking and laughing with the other members of our unit. We would watch the kids playing toy soldiers and realize that that was us; that was what we were doing but on a larger scale.

I am a Southerner born and bred and I thrive at the opportunity to spread my Southern heritage at every place that it is still allowed. I was born in Richmond, Virginia and have lived my entire life in the South. I've read and studied the War of Northern Aggression since the day I began to read. The actions and beliefs of our Southern ancestors amaze me and should be passed on to future generations. Fortune has been with me in the many memorable experiences I have shared around the campfires and battlegrounds with some of the best Southern blood passed down by these brave people. This makes me proud. So why do I reenact? I don't; I live it! And there are not enough pages to explain why.

BATTLE OF BIG BETHEL - ENDVIEW PLANTATION, VIRGINIA 2005

CAPTAIN LEONARD RACE
Commanding Officer, Hampton's Legion 2nd, S.C.

It is not just the battles that interest reenactors. There was a lot of action before the war ever began and all of this is a part of our teaching history to our viewers. There was a forgotten political war with crucial turning points leading up to the Civil War. This too is a part of our history and that is what I will share:

In 1832 political differences between Democrats and National Republicans began to fester. Outrage over the Tariff of 1828 led South Carolina to secede and President Jackson readied troops for action. Henry Clay, however, proposed the Compromise Tariff of 1833, and the Civil War was prolonged thirty some years.

In 1851, a woman named Harriet Beecher Stowe was inspired to write a novel, originally published by excerpt in an anti-slavery newspaper, she titled *Uncle Tom's Cabin*. It publicly condemned slavery and paved the way for more anti-slavery literature that followed.

In 1859, John Brown, an abolitionist from Kansas, raided a federal arsenal at Harper's Ferry in Virginia. The raid resulted in the death of both his sons and six others. The attack, though it failed, hastened the onset of the Civil War.

It was not until 1860 that South Carolina seceded from the Union, followed by other states, to form the Confederate States of America. At this point, the Union had passed several opportunities to make changes that would preserve unity among the states.

On April 12th, 1861, the Confederate states fired upon Ft. Sumter, South Carolina, and this is known as the first shot of the Civil War.

Gettysburg, Pennsylvania 2005

CHRISTOPHER MARTIN GARLISS WITH SON
CHRISTOPHER BRIAN GARLISS

Reenacting is like taking a step back in time. It allows me to relate history to others, including my son, on a three-dimensional playing field.

Cedar Creek, Virginia 2005

ALAN-MICHAEL HONAKER
Knibb's Battery

I'm doing this to see what it was like back in the Civil War time, what my family did back then. I also like going to the ball dances like when I take Crystal to the dance. The people in Knibb's Battery are really close friends. I just like doing what I'm doing.

CRYSTAL MURRAY
Knibb's Battery

I've been reenacting ever since I was three, fifteen years now. I started out because my parents were, but I continued not only because it is fun but also because it builds relationships, builds character, and because of the historical value. The human interactions, smiles, fun, etc. are all priceless. It's awesome to see the tourists' reactions to the battles and camp life.

1st Manassas, Virginia 2005

WAR DOG
1ST LT. STEPHEN B. DUNN
4th VA Cavalry, Comp. D; Little Fork Rangers

My name is War Dog. I'm in the Fourth Virginia Cavalry D company, the Little Fork Rangers. We ride to further the Southern Cause. When I say Southern Cause I mean our Southern culture, our Southern traditions, our Southern sense of freedom. We ride to honor, and due to the respect of our ancestors who did the same thing. We also ride to protect and preserve that flag that people are trying to tear down with their false political correctness. This turkey is our camp mascot; 'camp meat' we call him. We've hung him in just about every camp we've had for many years now.

Cedar Creek, Virginia 2005

Terry Ryan, Knibb's Battery - Cedar Creek, Virginia 2006

Confederate Final Review - Secessionville, South Carolina

Joe Furguson's Cavalry - Kelly's Ford, Virginia 2005

Lexington, Virginia 2005

Lexington, Virginia 2005

RICK RIVIERE
Chesterfield Light Artillery

There's nothing like it. When we go out in the field and load up those guns and blast them; chills just go up my back. Makes me want to go out and howl at the moon. And then there is the comradery. Sitting around the fire at night listening to music and sharing stories, you'll never meet a finer group of people.

Cedar Creek, Virginia 2006

Knibb's Battery - Richmond, Virginia 2004

Col. Tony Farinelli, Chief of Artillery - Anv. Staff 2005

ARMY OF NORTHERN VIRGINIA - 1ST DIVISION STAFF, VIRGINIA 2005
Top Row: Left to Right: Maj. Jake Jannette, Col. Joe Pereira, Capt. Doc Harris, Col. Tony Farinelli, Gen. Bob Tolar, Lt. Col. Abe Wiles, Maj. James Stine.
Middle Row: Capt. Neville Watts, Lt. Col. Jimmy Cochrane, Col. Raymond Justice, Maj. Andy Franklin, Maj. Lynn Bull. **Bottom Row:** Col. Donny Taylor, 2nd Lt. Ken Sewell

Jim Choate as General George Pickett at Dixie Days - Mechanicsville, Virginia

CAROL JENKINS
1st Peninsula, Artillery

Reenacting is all those games you played as a child and those swashbuckling classes you took in school, then add those nights you spent singing around a campfire with your friends.

These people exhibit the best of qualities, therefore a joy to be around. They don't get money or fame, but they get to play.

Our unit galvanizes, which means we play North or South. To us it's not about who wins, it's about the portrayal, how well you do your job, feeling those guns come alive and knowing that it was partly your doing. After all, it never mattered who was the cowboy and who was the Indian.

Some of us have Civil War ancestor blood running through our veins. People who served and probably influenced our desire to reenact.

My relative was a surgeon from the Gee family. He taught his wife who didn't go to school and she fairly surpassed him, at least on the plantation in old Virginia. Lt. Russell Jenkins hails from the Jenkins's Brigade, all the same family from Sperryville, Virginia.

LEXINGTON, VIRGINIA 2005

Kelly's Ford, Virginia 2005

NUNS IN BATTLE

The nuns of Cedar Creek are members of Co. H, 119NYV. We portray nuns at battle reenactments to bring honor to those brave women, over 600 from twenty-three different orders. They earned the esteem and gratitude of Protestants and Catholics alike for the sacrifices and dedication they showed as nurses during the Civil War to both Union and Confederate soldiers.

Cedar Creek, Virginia 2004

1ST SGT. RICK MILLER, NATHAN SHOEMAKE AND CAPT. BILL RUSSELL, CEDAR CREEK, VIRGINIA

Col. Dan Shoemake, 1st Manassas, Virginia 2005

Col. Dave Cornett, 2nd Battalion, Longstreet Corps Infantry - "Johnny Rebs" - Gettysburg, Pennsylvania 2005

Captain Eric Koff
4th Virginia, Company D

Captain of the 4th Virginia company D, major of Stuart Hampton Squadron…

  I'm so glad that the Confederacy lost because the Confederacy is such a weak government, and America is so strong. I love my government so very much. I'll do just about anything for them as long as they let me be free and do what I want, I'll help them in any way I can. So the Southern Cause is the cause of it all.

LEXINGTON, VIRGINIA 2005

COL. RAYMOND C. JUSTICE
Army of Northern Virginia,
Chief of Staff

The reason I reenact is to preserve the memory of those that have gone before us. My ancestor was a Federal soldier, I usually portray a Confederate, but I have a Federal impression as well. I don't mind doing both, to portray both sides of this conflict to the public. I enjoy the companionship of my comrades. It is a great hobby that my uncle, Don Patterson, got me into sixteen years ago and I have enjoyed it ever since. My first and best experience was as a private at the 130th Wilderness. We were down going through the wilderness at six o'clock in the morning, around the Plank Road area. The fog hung in and all of a sudden all the woods was quiet. Then the guns opened up. The Federal infantry came out of nowhere and scared the bejeezus out of us. It felt so real to see the people take the hits in mass confusion and chaos. It was one of the best experiences I've ever had; it was so real that I felt like I was there in May 1864, at Orange Plank Road.

BATTLE OF BIG BETHEL - ENDVIEW PLANTATION, VIRGINIA 2005

**GREGORY AND ROBERTA RANDALL WITH
DAUGHTER KATELYN ELIZABETH RANDALL**
(Quote by Katelyn Randall)

I like to reenact because it's fun to dress up and get your picture taken. It's also fun to watch the war. When I am sixteen, I can't wait to go on the cannons and be a nurse because I'm going to be on the battlefield.

Jefferson Davis Dedication - Hollywood Cemetery - Richmond, Virginia 2004

TIM SMITH
Confederate Artillery Camp

The reason I believe in the Southern Cause is I am a Confederate states patriot, in the service of the just and honorable cause of the South, on behalf of the citizens of the Confederate States of America. It is my purpose and mission, to reclaim the honor of our forefathers who fought, suffered, bled, and died in our nation's defense. Unfurl and raise our Confederate States national flag to its rightful place in glory. Duty, responsibility and my own personal honor require of me to do whatever is lawful, peaceful, and honorable, in order to restore the Confederate States constitution to power, reseat the Confederate States government and the Confederate States of America to its rightful independence.

Gettysburg, Pennsylvania 2005

GREGORY RANDALL / STONEWALL JACKSON, 1ST MANASSAS, VIRGINIA 2005

Burning of Aiken, South Carolina 2005

DWIGHT NESBITT
Lt. Col. 1st Div. Army of Northern Virginia
Artillery Staff

The reason I reenact is to honor my great-great grandfather. I believe anyone who portrays a Southern soldier or civilian of that time should try his or her best to honor them by acting as they would have in the 1860s. When I put on that uniform, I become a soldier of that era. I would like to think my grandfather would be proud of me for trying to be a good soldier and obeying orders.

There have been many times when I have been at an event that I felt that my grandfather was with me, standing by my side watching over me. Many of the battlefields on which he fought are the same battlefields where I now reenact. Walking on the same grounds, and maybe standing in the same spot, makes me proud and honored and sometimes very humble and sad. The Southern soldier and civilians believed in their hearts they were doing the right thing. They had determination, spirit, courage and a strong belief in God. They felt that they could win the war.

There are times when we reenact that we may be disturbing and attracting ghosts from the past. It is like the quote from the book *Ghost Riders*, "Things that look like things are likely to attract the real things."

I look just like my grandfather and it makes me feel sometimes that I have been reincarnated, but who really knows?! So I will continue doing my best to honor him and carry on the Southern Cause. I love the South and I am very proud that I am of Southern heritage. God bless the South and the Southern soldiers that believed in their hearts they could win the war.

Battle Of Big Bethel - Endview Plantation, Virginia 2006

MARION TURNER
Knibb's Battery

This is my heritage, and I feel I have the right to remember the history of those times without someone getting their "nose bent out of shape." I have fun playing dress up also.

However, the living history is the most important part. There are too many adults and children alike that have not been exposed to the history of the American Civil War—The War Between the States—except very one-sided. We can remember, respect, and be glad we live in a great country—the USA.

Appomattox, Virginia 2004

BUDDY, ALICE, AND JOYCE COOK
BUDDY COOK, SGT.
Knibb's Battery, Southern Scot's Light Artillery

This is my culture; this is who I am. I have always been fascinated with the old ways and where my people came from, how they lived. They were mountain folk from western Virginia, Scots, Irish, Germans, English. They came here in colonial times as indentured servants and fought in the Revolution for freedom to begin a new life. For this they were paid with land in the wilderness, land that they cleared and plowed and built on and turned into a new way of life that was hard but good and they cherished it. They went to war when called upon to defend what they had from an invading army that threatened to take it away.

I have always been interested in how things were done in that time; watching my grandma milk cows, churn butter, kill, clear and fry a chicken on a wood stove. They worked hard and loved the Lord, their families and neighbors.

I have done this since I was eight years old, wearing a Confederate gray uniform, trimmed in artillery red and shooting my Johnny Reb cannon. I do it to honor those ancestors and to somehow discover the mystery of their life, how they did things, why they did things. It tells me who I am.

JOYCE COOK
Knibb's Battery

I find I have an inner quiet when I step into the shoes of another time. It's like the cares of this world drop away as I move into another time and what's left is what is truly important: family, friends, honor, and duty.

ALICE COOK
Knibb's Battery

It's fun!!

Huguenot Springs Dedication, Virginia 2005

UNKNOWN SOLDIERS

On April 2, 2005, four unknown North Carolina soldiers were buried with full military honors in Hollywood Cemetery. Lost for nearly one hundred forty years on the battlefield on which they gave their lives for the capitol of their nation, the soldiers were found by a relic hunter in the exact spot where they fell in battle. They were paraded past the statues of the great generals Lee, Stuart, Jackson, and President Davis in the annual Confederate Heritage Parade down Monument Avenue. They were then put to rest where so many of their comrades had been laid to rest before them.

Compiled by Melissa Christenson

Confederate Heritage Parade, Hollywood Cemetery, Virginia 2005

BURIAL OF FOUR NORTH CAROLINA SOLDIERS

Salute to the Widows At Burial of Four North Carolina Soldiers

Gary Allen

The states that seceded did not commit any crime; they did what they could by the Constitution. If the Northern states would not have invaded the South and taxed them unfairly if you will, they would not have left the United States. In doing what President Lincoln did, what would you have done? Would you A) sit back and let them tax you the same way that Britain taxed America before the Revolutionary War, as well as let them invade you? Or would you B) practice your rights of secession and secede, not accepting an unfair tax. No, the war was not fought over slavery; it was fought over states' rights. Slavery was not an issue until Britain had 15,000 troops in Canada ready to push New York. Then and only then did Lincoln make slavery an issue to save the U.S. You hear people say that we fired upon Fort Sumter, but it was the Union that fired on Sumter, which was actually South Carolina's property. So after that, South Carolina seceded. Lincoln was wrong throughout the war, even before it had truly started. Maryland was going to secede but Lincoln put the whole Maryland legislature in jail and appointed a legislature that would not secede. The way the Union fought the war was satanic, if you will. They burned and pillaged Southern homes while raping Southern women and children. The Union continued this way throughout the entire war. This is why I know that the South was right.

Col. W. H. Taylor
A.K.A. Gary Allen

Hunter's Raid - Lexington, Virginia 2005

Buck Shaw

Well, I grew up in rural Arkansas, and at that time back in the sixties, if you didn't have a Confederate flag flying somewhere around your house, people wondered what was wrong with you. I noticed this as I was growing up and especially over the last ten years, that it's really starting to disappear, that it's going away, it's being washed out of our society. That does bother me. I was a military officer, an army officer, for the better part of thirteen years, in the regular army of the United States. One of the first things I encountered there was that if you wanted to be accepted in that society, you did not display your heritage, you could not be a Southerner, which I found to be somewhat of a dichotomy because the military has always been made up of Southern officers. We have our heritage from way back, all the way back to the Revolution. So I learned some interesting lessons there. I left the army in 1992. In 1994 I started law school at the University of Arkansas at Little Rock. If you read things and you go to a class and things are being taught that are just a little strange, and don't agree with the things you read, the red flag goes up. All these interesting stories about how white men went into Africa, the deepest darkest part of Africa and captured these people and took them slaves, which is not true. They bought them, right there on the west coast of Africa. What fascinates me there is that we have people now wanting reparations from the United States government for slavery. Why are they not going back to the Africans and asking for reparations from the people who sold their ancestors into slavery? Why is that not happening? Are they going to deny that part of their history? Why is it when you go to a place like Branson, Missouri, which used to be like the Confederate capitol of the world, you can't even find a Confederate flag anymore to buy as a souvenir? Are we going to deny our heritage, deny what we are? People are so upset because slavery existed under the Confederate flag for four years, what about the other flag it existed under for ninety years? There are some things we need to ask ourselves. What bothers me about all this is that we've entered a time when everyone is expected to identify with something. You can't simply be an American anymore; you have to be an African-American or an Indian-American, or you have to be an Irish-American or you have to be a Chinese-American and all this. Everybody's hyphenated, but you can not in this culture anymore recognize your Southern heritage. Southern Americans, some of us, a lot of us, that's as far back as our heritage goes.

The South didn't want to fight for control of the government, they just wanted to break off and do their own thing. States rights, interesting thing, when you take a course like constitutional law, what do you get? You learn about something called federalism. You have the federal government and the state government and they are constantly at each others' throats, either under the surface, or on the surface, it makes little difference. Back then they were at it on the surface, now they say well we settled this issue, maybe we didn't, because the states still look around and say hey we want to do this, we want to control that and the federal government says we're going to stay in your business. That's what this war was all about. That's what these issues were about. I've heard the historians say that if the South had known what the issues were going to be, they would have probably never agreed to go along with the revolution in the first place. They wanted the states to have individual rights. Was it the best form of government? Possibly not, but we lived under that government for several years under the Articles of Confederation. Articles of Confederation, what was it? It was a Confederacy, and the right to secede was there; they thought it was there. We look at this and then we look at the Reconstruction years, oh well gee you never left the Union, well I guess you did now because we're going to make it very difficult for you to come back. The hardships that people experienced over this, you know, Southerners hated Lincoln; Lincoln was a friend of the South. If he'd lived, I think we would have seen a very different Reconstruction, but unfortunately he did not. Sherman; everybody hates Sherman. Sherman was a great man. He fought war like war should be fought and when it was all over he said ok it's over, let's go home. Let's go home and rebuild a country and let's quit fighting now. That's the way he saw it. That's why he was the one who said, when they wanted him to run for president, "If nominated, I will not run, if elected I will not serve." That was a great man. He fought his war and then he went home. He said let's forget it.

POCAHONTAS PARK, VIRGINIA

Major Tony Lackey
Army of Northern Virginia, Artillery Staff
Ordnance Pvt. of Chesterfield Light Artillery

I do reenactments in honoring other people and my ancestors. I believe in the Southern Cause because it's what they believed in. My great-great grandfather was Thomas S. Galloway and he was a colonel in the 22nd North Carolina Infantry and he was with General Lee at Appomattox, Virginia. After the war was over, he moved to Tennessee to fulfill his profession as a lawyer.

The Southerners fought for what they believed in and it wasn't about slavery. It was about states' rights. Most of the Southerners couldn't afford slaves, hell, none of my ancestors had slaves. Another reason why I reenact is to show people in the United States and other countries that Americans fought against Americans. It was a cold and brutal war but a gentlemen's war. Southerners mostly fought for what they believed in, the North fought because they didn't have any other choice but to fight.

If there was to be another war between the states, I would bear arms for my state and for what I believe to be just as they did. It's not about people, it's about a way of life. I would definitely support North Carolina and South Carolina, my two home states. I have people come to me and ask me why I reenact when the South lost the war. I don't look at it like that. I look at it as heritage and history. I reenact on both sides, North as well as South, to show that it is not about hate but about American heritage and history. The people against the South and the battle flag, in my opinion, should grow up and get on with it because you can not change history. History will always be there. The government is trying to do away with the battlefields rather than preserving them for their historical value. They would rather have the taxes and the revenue that comes off the property that is sold. If it weren't for some states trying to preserve these battlefields, this part of our history would be lost. History would only be in our hearts and souls, so GOD BLESS DIXIELAND AND THE SOUTHERN CAUSE!

Cedar Creek, Virginia 2005

Cynthia DiCarlo, mrs cuz
Army of Northern Virginia
Staff, Longstreet Corps

Our primary mission is serving as staff to the commanding generals of Longstreets Corps. Stephen is the flag bearer and I serve as guard. We also participate with the Army of Northern Virginia Cavalry. (We were portraying cavalry troopers in the pics at Kelly's Ford.)

Our full names are Cynthia DiCarlo and Stephen DiCarlo (alias Cuz). We are known in reenacting as Cindy and Cuz. Stephen's friend Charles Hillsman, the first commanding general of Longstreets Corps, reenactment group, got him started in reenacting about eighteen years ago and he has been known as Cuz ever since.

Stephen has a very direct connection with the Civil War. He grew up with many stories of the hardships that his family endured during those last days before the surrender. His family once owned Hillsman Farm, now known as the Saylers (Sailors) Creek battlefield near Amelia, Virginia. His great-great-great grandfather was a captain in the Confederate army and one of the Immortal 600. His grandmother was at the farm during the battle where she provided food and helped bury the dead after the battle. He remembers his grandmother giving tours of the Hillsman Farm, seeing bloodstains on the floor. (The house was used as a hospital during the battle).

I don't have any direct ancestors to brag about, but started my reenacting career based on my love of the 19th century culture (thanks to watching *Gone with the Wind* as a child). My first Civil War impression was very civilian, demonstrating quilting and spinning wool. Next, I portrayed a woman in full mourning. My third was that of a male contract Confederate working at general's mess. Lastly, I am portraying a cavalry trooper.

Why do we reenact? For the love of history and to get away from the 21st century. Most importantly, to enjoy the great friendships within our "family" of reenactors.

Pocahontas Park, Virginia

STEPHEN DICARLO
Army of Northern Virginia
Staff, Longstreet Corps

Stephen 'Cuz' DiCarlo, ANV Staff, Longstreet Corps - Pocahontas Park, Virginia

STACEY WEHMEYER
Knibb's Battery, Vivandiere

Peeling away the layers of my modern mentalities and clothing, I pack it all away in an antique trunk. Placing my feather-plumed hat on my head and my gun in my belt, I now have replaced my identity and transformed into what one calls "living history." I am a lady in the 1800s; I am a vivandiere.

Come step back in a time when the men are gentlemen and the women are ladies. Each is treated with their due respect. Ladies dress in the fineries of lace and petticoats, frilly satin gowns, and walk with heads held high. Men walk in uniform with the look of great patriotic pride. One can walk by strangers yet get recognition by a tipped hat or a nod of one's head, followed by a, "Good day to you, madam, or sir." One will see strangers helping one another, out of the sense of honor and pride. Hands held out not for payment for their deeds but for a grateful handshake of thanks.

As a reenactor, I am the book one reads. I am the movie people watch. I have become (I AM) history. So as to portray the person, to relive the past, to teach what my ancestors experienced: from the way they dressed, lived, acted, and fought

We go without showers for days, we live among the bugs and snakes. Sweat in the blazing hot sun, and shiver in our tents from the bitter cold. But we also camp under the beauty of a star-filled night, listen to simple but good old-time music, and sit around the night's campfire swapping stories of the historical pasts of our ancestors. It is an escape for us from the hustle and bustle of our real lives…and for what? It is all for the preservation, the remembering, the honoring of our forefathers of a time gone by but not to be forgotten.

Whether on the battlefield firing cannons, living among the troops, or going from being sweaty, dirty, and tired from the day's battles, to clean up the best we can, putting on our fineries and waltzing away the evening at the ball…it is all very emotional for me. Knowing that we are just playing dress up and just playing war, when in fact knowing that it was all very real long ago…and that we did fight. And that we did fight against our friends, neighbors, even family…for unity!

So for all of you spectators and fellow reenactors, let us not forget our ancestors who fought for us, for unity. We are one nation under God!

GETTYSBURG, PENNSYLVANIA 2005

POCAHONTAS PARK, VIRGINIA 2005

Endview plantation, Virginia 2005

RICK AND MEGAN BARDEN
(Megan)

Spending time with my father can be the most fun. When the men start the fire and the beans are being eaten, it's like *Blazing Saddles*!

Appomattox, Virginia 2004

AMANDA DHAUP
5th VA Cavalry Comp. H

I started reenacting in 1998 as a woman and I researched my family and found out that several of them were in the 1st VA cavalry and 4th VA cavalry. I was convinced to then start riding, I have been riding all my life. I got into the cavalry side of it which I enjoy. The worst experience was breaking a few bones here and there; the best being that I get to come out here and have a great time with all my friends. I have a blast doing it. Being a woman in the cavalry is pretty hard but it is extremely wonderful and everybody is real accommodating and helps me all they can. I have learned a whole lot about the Civil War since I started and now I am addicted. Also I enjoy being able to come out here and have a great time while honoring my heritage. I have twenty members of my family that I can directly link that were in the Civil War, all were Virginians and all were Confederates. I am proud to be out here to honor them.

Battle of Big Bethel - Endview Plantation, Virginia 2005

Knibb's Battery - Cedar Creek, Virginia 2006

Gettysburg, Pennsylvania 2005

Burning of Aiken, South Carolina 2005

Gettysburg, Pennsylvania 2006

WALLY HUDGINS

Because my grandfather was a Confederate soldier and his brother was a Confederate officer, I was born a son of the Confederacy. As I grew and matured, I learned more about my grandfather from my father. To this day, I cherish some of my grandfather's personal belongings from that time period, more specifically his worn pocket watch. I became what some call a "Civil War Buff." The more I learned and experienced, the more I wanted to learn and experience about any and everything I could regarding the War Between the States.

I held an application to join The Sons of Confederate Veterans (SCV) in my possession for many years. After finally joining the SCV and learning more about the history of various battles, etc., I was introduced to Knibb's Battery. A future compatriot, who allowed me to wear his uniform on a temporary basis, invited me to participate in an upcoming memorial event at Hollywood Cemetery. Once experiencing firsthand the excitement of what it might have felt like during 1861-1865, I was hooked. Being a member of the battery provides me with a more personal and real connection with my ancestry. It also provides a relationship with other compatriots within the battery where we all have a common bond; our past and the cause for which our Southern ancestors so proudly fought for what they felt was right for them and their families. Without our ancestors and what they represented, we as descendants would not be who we are today.

Thus, I am a member of Knibb's Battery to honor my grandfather.

Jefferson Davis Dedication - Hollywood Cemetery, Virginia 2004

PAULETTE NESBITT
Chesterfield Light Artillery

For Love! Love of my husband, the outdoors, gathering around the campfires, the fellowship, the dressing in period attire, the shopping, the people, the history of my country and my state, my ancestors and what they went through, the horses, learning history and teaching to others what I have learned. These things put together still can't say it all.

Each new day is a learning experience and a way I can honor my ancestors who fought so hard and so gallantly for their state's rights. As a reenactor, I am able to experience the hardships my ancestors endured. It is like traveling back to a time when the pace of life was much slower. We live as our ancestors lived; cooking over open fires, sleeping in tents, with no control over the elements. Sometimes I can't help but wonder, "Why in the world am I doing this?" Then I encounter curious spectators that I am able to share what I have learned with; or we are encamped beside a lake or in a beautiful pastoral setting or beside a gorgeous plantation, it seems to make it all worthwhile.

I have been certified as a cannoneer. I dress as a Confederate artillery soldier and shoot the cannon by my husband's side. Normally I serve on a mountain howitzer or a mountain rifle since they are both smaller guns and I am rather short. This men's attire is not the least bit becoming and I prefer dressing as a lady. It is always fun to dress up and shop for new things to add to my wardrobe. We attend fashion shows, teas, and balls. The ladies are treated with much respect, much as they were before, during and after the Civil War. The gentlemen smile and tip their hats and offer their arm in escort. The spectators and their children also smile and ask questions such as, "Aren't you hot in all those clothes?" I smile back and answer truthfully, "Yes, it is rather hot and I am truly glad these are not mourning garments, for they are much warmer." All the experience is a pleasure.

Cedar Creek, Virginia 2006

PRIVATE J.L. MARLOW

The best memory of when I fully realized I was destined to become involved with reenactments, battlefield preservation, memorial sevices and the many other causes relating to our Southern heritage, came one hot humid summer day in August. We, my wife, mother-in-law, and children, were watching the annual Peanut Festival parade held in Brooklet, Georgia. About thirty minutes into the event you could hear the distinct sound of the drum and fife and occasional musket volley heading our way. The hairs stood on the back of my neck and goose bumps ran down my legs as the Sons of Confederate Veterans marched so proudly by, seemingly unaware of the drenching heat. The rest is history.

All along I've known that I am a "Son of the South," but until that moment I never understood the responsibility that comes with being "a Son" really means. Long live the South!

1st Manassas, Virginia 2006

BRIAN SOLES

I am Brian Soles; I am a bugler. I have an original bugle that has been in my family for many years, since the Civil War. I found it in my granddad's attic. It belonged to his great-great grandfather who was with the 7th Virginia Cavalry. My granddaddy used to tell me stories about it but I don't know too much. I started reenacting oh, I say about fifteen or sixteen years ago. I started off with the 35th Cavalry, went to 7th Virginia Cavalry, Company F and I moved away for awhile but then moved back. Now I am with Knibb's Battery doing artillery and I enjoy it. You know, you can get a lot of people out here and have a lot of fun. I enjoy it, I can't stay away from it. I just love it, I meet a lot of new people. Everybody is usually friendly with everybody else. We all are out here to have fun and to preserve part of our history. We are trying to keep these developers from taking away our history, so our children, grandchildren and so forth, when they get older, they'll know at least a small part of our history. Thank you for this time, I appreciate the photos.

CEDAR CREEK, VIRGINIA 2006

LET US SAY A PRAYER FOR ALL WHO DIED FOR "THE CAUSE"

Knowing in our hearts that if any good came from such a mighty loss, it did indeed restore our nation's declaration that all men are created equal. Bow your heads, for they died to keep the Southern Cause honored and alive and achieved in death that which could never be achieved in life: IMMORTALITY!

Long Live Dixie,
Long Live the Southern Cause,
Long Live the United States of America!

by Thomas A. Daniel

Surrender Prayer - Appomattox, Virginia 2006

NUMBERS AND LOSSES

	North	South[1]
Population	22,400,000	9,103,000[2]
Military Age Group (18-45)	4,600,000	985,000
Trained Militia 1827-1861	2,470,000	692,000
Regular Army January, 1861	16,400	0
Military Potential 1861	2,486,400	692,000
Total Individuals in Service 1861-1865	2,213,400	1,003,600
Total Strength, July, 1861	219,400	114,000
Total Strength, January, 1863	962,300	450,200
Peak Strength, 1864-1865	1,044,660	484,800
Army	980,100	481,200
Navy	60,700	3,000
Marines	3,860	600
Total Hit in Battle	385,100	320,000
Total Battle Deaths	110,100	94,000
Killed in Battle	67,100	54,000
Died of Wounds	43,000	40,000
Wounded (not mortally)[3]	275,000	226,000
Missing in Action	6,750	---
Captured[4]	211,400	462,000
Died in Prison	30,200	26,000
Died of Disease	224,000	60,000
Other Deaths	34,800	---
Desertions[5]	199,000	83,400
Discharged	426,500	57,800
Surrendered 1865		174,223

1. Confederate figures are based upon the best information and estimates available.
2. Includes 3,760,000 slaves in the seceded states.
3. A number of these were returned to duty. In the Union Army, those who were not fit for combat were placed in the Veteran Reserve Corps and performed administrative duties.
4. An undetermined number were exchanged and returned to duty.
5. Many deserters returned to duty. In the Union Army, where $300 bounty was paid for a 3-year enlistment, it was not uncommon to find a soldier picking up his bounty in one regiment and deserting to join another unit just for the additional bounty.

Civil War Handbook, Price, William H. L.B. Prince Co., 1961.